Quick and Easy Crafts

Beadwork

Quick and Easy Crafts

Beadwork

15 step-by-step projects – simple to make, stunning results

ROBIN BELLINGHAM,
HANA GLOVER & JEMA HEWITT

NEW
HOLLAND

First published in 2004 by
New Holland Publishers (UK) Ltd
London · Cape Town · Sydney · Auckland

Garfield House, 86–88 Edgware Road, London W2 2EA, United Kingdom
www.newhollandpublishers.com

80 McKenzie Street, Cape Town 8001, South Africa

Level 1, Unit 4, 14 Aquatic Drive, Frenchs Forest, NSW 2086, Australia

218 Lake Road, Northcote, Auckland, New Zealand

ISBN 1 84330 691 3

Senior Editor: Clare Sayer
Production: Hazel Kirkman
Design: AG&G Books Glyn Bridgewater
Photographer: Shona Wood
Editorial Direction: Rosemary Wilkinson

10 9 8 7 6 5 4 3 2 1

Reproduction by Pica Digital Pte Ltd, Singapore
Printed and bound by Times Offset (M) Sdn Bhd, Malaysia

Acknowledgements

*Hana would like to thank Richard for helping us start The Bead Shop in the first place. Sarah for all her
support. Becca and Dave for testing the projects. Hannah in Oz for all the help and inspiration she has given.
Last and not least all the staff at The Bead Shop (Jo, Rosie, Jema, Jenette, Angela, Becky and Sophie) for all
of their hard work in helping us keep to our business plan and grow the shop to what it is today because
without it we would never have been approached to do this book.*
*Jema would like to thank Lynn Hardy for her support and enthusiasm and for first tempting me with beads
and teaching me the beading stitches! Nik Hewitt – my wonderful husband for happily putting up with
beads EVERYWHERE and showing me how to use a computer. My Mum and Dad for always having loads of
exciting creative oddments lying about, and encouraging me to play with them.*
*Robin would like to thank Jill – Mum, this is for you to show all those to whom you may have been
embarrassed to admit that one of your sons makes a living from beads. Thanks for never getting in the way
of whatever I've wanted to do.*

Contents

 Projects

Introduction

Beads have been in use for 40,000 years, originally a part of religious rites and ceremonies, and as currency up until the colonization of the Americas. The beauty of beads today is that you can use them to create a stunning item of jewellery to complement any outfit, or a fantastic personal gift, in either a little or a long time. A simple design can take just two hours to complete, or a more absorbing project may take many evenings' work. Whichever it is, the results are sure to be spectacular.

The projects included in this book have been graded in terms of difficulty, from the simple to the more complicated, but each is also a stand-alone project. You may wish to go through the projects one by one, or pick out a particular project that's caught your eye, either way we're sure you'll enjoy the whole creative process.

Once you have started to experiment with beads your knowledge of beading will grow, along with your collection of beads, very rapidly. Don't be afraid to buy beads that you like the look of, even if you are not sure what you are going to do with them. The ideas will come to you, especially at unlikely times, and it's always useful to have a good selection of beads at hand for when they do.

We hope you have fun with the ideas and projects in this book, and experiment with them to your own specifications. The same project can look very different when different shapes, sizes and colours of beads are used. Use your creativity and don't forget there is no wrong way to go with beads.

Materials

There is a fantastic range of beads to be found, along with a number of specialist threads to arrange them on and jewellery findings to finish the piece. If you don't have a bead shop or quality craft shop in your area, never fear, because everything you need can be bought mail order or on the internet.

Beads

Beads are available in so many different colours, shapes and sizes that it is often difficult to know where to start when choosing them. In the projects in this book we have given guidance as to the type of beads you will need and given quantities where appropriate but you are much more likely to buy beads in pre-packed quantities, rather than in specific numbers. Don't worry if you can't find exactly the same size or colour that we have used as many of the projects can be made up with your own choice of beads.

Seed beads, also known as rocailles, are tiny round glass beads. They are available in a range of numbered sizes – confusingly, the higher the number the smaller the bead. The size is often written as 10/0 or 10°. Sizes between 15 (tiny) and 5 (large) are commonly available, and the most commonly used sizes are 10 and 11. Seed beads can be found in a huge variety of colours and finishes and are also manufactured in different shapes, such as cylinders, hexagons and triangles. They are manufactured mainly in the Czech Republic and Japan, with lower quality versions also made in China and India. Czech seed beads tend to be round, and Japanese seed beads have larger holes and are more cylindrical and consistent in shape.

Crystal beads and bicones are available in a myriad of colours and finishes, the most popular being the AB or Aurora Borealis finish. Crystal beads are machine-cut to produce sparkling facets. They are available in a tremendous range of shapes including bicone, round and cube beads. I find the bicone the most versatile crystal shape to use. Crystal pendants are also available in shapes such as crosses, drops and hearts.

Pressed glass beads are formed from molten glass pressed between two moulds. Adding oxides to the glass before it is pressed creates the colours. Pressed glass beads come in many shapes, such as cubes, ovals, flowers and leaves. Pressed faceted beads are an inexpensive alternative to cut glass or crystal beads. The many colours and finishes available, such as frosted and Aurora Borealis (AB), make these a very popular type of bead.

Venetian beads are handmade glass beads created by "lamp work", where a glass rod is formed into a bead and worked over a special torch. The beads are created in layers and exquisitely decorated. Venice has been a centre for glass beadmakers since Renaissance times. Techniques for making and working glass were shrouded in mystery and the secrets of the Italian craftsmen were kept for hundreds of years.

Kiln-made glass beads are made by winding heated glass, not quite molten, around a steel rod before being pressed in a metal mould to form the shape. Indian glass beads are often characterized by the hole having a chalky residue, this is because a thin layer of clay is used on the steel rod to prevent the bead from sticking. Indian glass beads are mostly handmade in varying size workshops.

Bugle beads are long, cylindrical beads, the tubular version of seed beads. They are available in much the same colours and finishes as seed beads, with sizes ranging from 2–30 mm in length. Bugles can be round or hexagonal in shape. Twisted bugles are formed from twisting the hexagonal tubes while the glass is molten and before they are cut into bugles.

Delica or Treasure Beads are the trade names for precision-made Japanese cylindrical seed beads. They have relatively large holes and are consistent in size and shape so they fit together perfectly when woven, making them ideal for beadweaving.

Semiprecious beads such as amethyst, garnet, lapis lazuli and turquoise are very beautiful and add value to a special piece of jewellery. Many stones are available both as round beads, carved and faceted shapes, as well as the irregular tumblechips. Some stones are marked out as "birthstones" while others are alleged to impart good fortune or feelings to their owners, which can add meaning to a present.

Pearls are nature's classic gems, created by the humble oyster. Natural pearls are fantastically rare, and most real pearls are now cultivated. Many shapes are available, from the affordable tiny rice grain and irregular baroque, to the extremely expensive perfect round pearl. Assorted colours are also found naturally, including the famous black pearl. Others can be dyed. Wonderful fake pearl beads are also available in varying degrees of quality and realism, but the real thing is always obvious.

Antique beads are stunning one-of-a-kind art pieces, but so also are many modern beads. From hand-rolled felt beads and hand-carved semiprecious to iridescent dichroic lamp-worked one-offs, some beads simply cannot be mass-produced. One gorgeous handmade bead can create a perfect focus for a necklace, as well as becoming an heirloom in its own right in years to come. Look out for local artists as well as exciting finds while travelling abroad.

Bali beads are traditionally handmade sterling-silver beads with intricate designs created on the bead surface using sterling silver wire.

Plastic beads are available in a much larger range of colours and effects than any other type of bead, including glow-in-the-dark and neon, which makes these beads inexpensive and fun to use. Most plastic beads are produced in the USA or China.

Wooden beads are a popular choice. Wood is incredibly versatile because it can be carved, varnished or stained. Beads can be made from many different types of wood, each of which has a natural beauty, often enhanced by a simple coat of varnish. Wooden beads are available in many shapes, sizes and bright colours.

Natural beads, like shells, are readily available on a beach near you, as are other natural sources such as seeds and acorns. Be careful not to break them when making a hole for threading. This is the only drawback to using these "free" beads. Bone is

another material that is popular for making beads, usually made from cattle bone, these beads can be carved, painted or dyed.

Polymer clay is a wonderfully versatile medium for creating beads and pendants. It is soft, like clay, until it is baked in an ordinary oven. Although it is a relatively new medium, there are many wonderful artists constantly inventing new techniques for making beads and pendants with it. Incredible effects can be achieved with it, from millefiori to faux semiprecious stones, with very little needed in the way of specialist equipment.

Threads and wires

The material you thread your beads on depends on the type of project you are creating. There are a whole range of options available.

Beading thread is a very strong polyester thread that is primarily used to hang semiprecious beads and stones. This is because of the weight of the beads, and because older and lower quality semiprecious beads tend to have sharp edges around the hole, which can go through thread very quickly. Beading thread is found in a few colours and from sizes 0.4 mm (27 SWG) to 0.8 mm (21 SWG). It needs to be cut with scissors.

Nymo is a strong but very thin nylon thread originally used in the manufacture of clothing and upholstery coverings. As a thin, strong thread, Nymo was adopted by the beading world because it is ideal for projects that involve passing through beads several times, or passing through very small beads

like Delicas. The most popular and widely available size is D. Other gauges are available and the choice of colours is excellent.

Silamide is a waxed thread that is slightly thicker than Nymo and available in brighter colours. It is also ideal for beadweaving.

Monofilament is a plastic unstranded thread, rather like nylon fishing wire. It is very strong and is often used in Japanese-style beadweaving crystal projects or "floating" necklaces. It is available in an assortment of widths and is usually transparent or black. Although it is not stretchy as such, it does have a bit of "give", so is unsuitable for heavy beads threaded in a simple strand.

Plated wires usually have a copper core that has been plated either silver or gold. The most frequently used diameters range from 0.2 mm (32 SWG) through to 1.6 mm (14 SWG). This kind of wire is used in making handmade jewellery findings and link chains. The smaller gauges are not suitable for stringing beads but the larger gauges can be used to make choker bands or tiara bases.

Tigertail is a very fine, plastic-coated metal cord. It is available in a range of colours and an assortment of stranded widths. Because of its metal core it is extremely tough, but it doesn't kink in the same way that wire does. Some softer brands can be knotted and manipulated like thread; others are stiffer and need crimps to fasten on necklace ends.

Stretch Magic was originally used in the clothing industry, but it was soon discovered by beaders as it is incredibly versatile and easy to use. As it expands to several times its be weaker than cotton bootlace and can be snapped with your hands. There are plenty of different threads available for stringing beads – the bead-hole size will dictate which you can and cannot use. Experiment and see which one you prefer.

Memory wire is used in all sorts of projects. It is very strong, hard wire that always reverts back to its original round shape, hence its name. It is available in a range of sizes. It needs to be cut with specialist pliers to however many coils are needed. The sharp ends can then be made into a loop or a bead cap glued in place and beads threaded on.

Jewellery findings

Findings are an important part of any jewellery project, and there are a number of options available.

Clasps are the finishing touch on a piece, from elaborate to simple, each has its place. Simple screw-together torpedo and barrel clasps are great on necklaces, but a nightmare to do up one-handed on a bracelet. Lobster clasps and bolt rings are very easy to use, use a jump ring as a loop for the other side. Special clasps are available for multi-stranded projects and it's always worth keeping some gold and sterling-silver clasps to hand for extra special designs.

Crimps are available in a variety of types, but the most common are tiny, metal, circular beads that are crushed against threads with pliers for securing. The crimp grips the thread and doesn't move. Tubular crimps tend to be neater when crushed and are a lot less likely to break the thread they are being crimped against. Crimps can also be used to

original length, no clasp is required. Just tie a couple of knots, you may even be able to hide the knot inside a bead. The fabric elastic has a rubber core and is now available in a few colours, other than black and white, and a limited number of gauges. Thinner plastic elastic is now widely available in lots of colours, including clear. Although not as strong as the fabric elastic, this elastic is suitable for seed beads and other small-holed beads. It requires at least three knots to secure it properly, and a dab of glue will always help.

Pearl threads are manmade fibres used for threading pearls. Traditionally pearls were threaded on pure silk strands to preserve their lustre. Specialist pearl cord is silky, which makes it easy to create and manipulate knots in. Some cords

even have needles ready threaded in the pack. Pearls are knotted to protect them from scratching or chipping each other, but an added bonus is that if the cord breaks you don't lose the whole precious strand.

Chains will transform a simple pendant into something really special, so it's worth keeping a few in your workbox for emergency presents. Chains are available in gold, silver and base metals, and are created by attaching links in various ways. Chain can also be measured off the roll for special projects.

Cotton strands are often plaited together to make a strong string for large-holed beads. It is sometimes referred to as bootlace.

Leather cord is available in similar gauges to cotton strand but not such a variety of colours. Leather tends to space beads out on a strand that can't be knotted – simply slide the crimp onto the thread and crush with a pair of thin-nose pliers. Use crimps either side of a bead to stop it moving on the thread and to space the bead from its neighbour. Crimps can also be used as a spacer bead, either on threads or an earring pin. They are also used at the end of a thread to attach a clasp.

Earring wires can be found in a range of shapes. Some look like a simple fishhook or kidney wire, while others have a post and butterfly back. Different front fittings take dangles or glue-on cabochons. When making earrings as gifts for friends remember that some people are allergic to base metal and can only wear gold or silver.

Headpins and eyepins are used for the majority of earring projects. The headpin has a flat end, which stops the beads from falling off the pin. The eyepin has a loop, which also stops beads from falling off the pin but gives you the advantage of either hanging another pin from the loop, making long earrings, or hanging a pendant below the beads. Both types of pin need to have a loop made at the top so that they can be hung from an earring wire.

Jump rings are a circular piece of small-gauge wire, which has a break in the loop so it can be twisted open. Jump rings are useful items to have to hand as they can change the orientation of a pendant or be used to link two closed loops together. Several jump rings together make an ideal safety chain for awkward clasps. Several diameters and shapes are available. Jump rings can be also be

handmade using plated wire and a pair of round-nose pliers.

Necklace ends are used to attach a clasp to the necklace cord. They are also sometimes called calottes or clamshells. Necklace ends can be side or end opening. The side openers have the thread entering from the side, whereas the end openers have the thread entering through the centre of the necklace end. These findings are used on smaller gauges of beadstring and can be attached by either tying a knot in the thread or using a crimp.

Spacer bars are essential for multi-stranded projects, because they keep the different layers separate and are threaded on as part of the design. Most common are those with three or five holes, but other sizes are available too. They can be found in gold and sterling silver as well as

plated metals, you can even find fabulous fancy ones to become a central feature of the design.

Thong ends are used for larger gauges of thread, usually 1 mm or larger. These work by inserting the thread into the end and crushing the last coil against itself, securing the thread by crimping. These are usually available as plated items. There is a loop at the end, which connects with the clasp. Thin cord is better secured when doubled over.

Triangular clamps are used when circular jump rings will not fit. This is generally when a hole is not close enough to the edge of the pendant or the pendant is especially wide. These clamps are better when hanging crystal pendants. They are open when you buy them, and when positioned correctly just need the legs pushing towards each other to grip.

Tools

To get started with any beadwork project, you will need a few basic tools. Some of these you may already have around the house or garage, while you may need to buy other, more specialist equipment. The following is a list of all the equipment you are likely to come across when making the projects in this book.

Bead design board

Bead design boards come in either a single or multi-strand configuration. Shallow channels in the board allow you to lay out the beads in a chosen pattern without having to re-thread the beads time and time again to see how the design looks. The channels stop rounded beads from moving out of line, making the pattern easy to see. Most boards have semicircular channels that have a unit of measure around the outer side to help you ascertain the length of your project.

Bead tray and mat

One useful piece of equipment for the beader is a tray and mat. The mat will stop the beads rolling all over the place. The tray allows you to keep all your beads and tools close to hand, and is a useful way to store and move your work without disrupting it.

Glue

Glue is used to space beads out along a thread. Other uses include stiffening or preventing fraying at the end of a thread, making threading without a needle easier, and securing knots so that they cannot work themselves undone, especially when

you least expect it. Fabric glues are good for porous threads, whereas superglue can be used on all threads, although it tends to be brittle and less controllable. We use special bead glue, available from most bead suppliers as it gives slightly better results.

Needles

Needles are an important tool when it comes to beadwork and it is a good idea to keep a selection in your workbox. Flexible beading needles are made from twisted wire and have a large, easily threaded eye that compresses to get through small beads. For beadweaving and embroidery a sharp beading needle is best. These are like normal sewing needles but much thinner. The eye is also thinner so a needle threader can be invaluable, or for thick cord try stiffening the end with a wrap of tape or dab of superglue.

Pliers

There are a variety of jewellery pliers available on the market. Some of these are specific tools for specific beading tasks. Round-nose pliers – both plier jaws are round – are used to make loops and spirals. Flat-nose pliers – both jaws are flat and, more importantly, smooth – are used for gripping and crimping. Some pliers come with a serrated surface. This does help with gripping but it can also mark and damage your work.

Reamer

Reamers have several attachments to enable you to clear or enlarge holes

in beads. Another attachment will smooth sharp edges where the thread enters and exits the bead. Mostly used with semiprecious beads, ceramics or glass.

Scissors and thread cutters

A small pair of very sharp embroidery scissors is invaluable. Only use them for thread, never paper or wire, which will blunt and chip them. Thread cutters are wonderful gadgets and are the only cutters allowed on airlines (just in case you like to do a little in-flight beading). A circular blade is completely encased in a decorative metal cover with tiny sections cut away, for a safe trimmer.

Wire cutters

Do not use scissors to cut wire, they will be ruined. Use wire cutters for all wire except memory wire, which is extremely strong and will wreck normal cutters very quickly. Special memory wire cutters are available.

Techniques

Beadwork does not involve a lot of complicated techniques, but there are a few basic skills you will need to learn. Although the projects have full step-by-step instructions, it is worth taking the time to familiarize yourself with the basics.

Necklace ends

Necklace ends all work in the same way – by covering a crimp or knot securing the necklace end to the thread. These findings are either side closing, end closing or cupped.

To use a side-closing necklace end
1 Tie a knot or crush a crimp with flat-nose pliers as close as possible to the last bead on the project.
2 Using the pliers, sit the knot or crimp in one cup and close the second cup onto the first.
3 Hook the metal tail of the necklace end onto a clasp and loop it back on itself. Repeat at the other end.

To use an end-closing necklace end
1 Thread the strand through the hole where the two cups of the necklace end fold. Crush a crimp with flat-nose pliers or tie a knot in the thread.

2 Use flat-nose pliers to close the two cups together, completely covering the crimp or knot.

3 Hook the metal tail of the necklace end onto a clasp and loop it back on itself. Repeat for the other end but fully open the necklace end so that the crimp or knot can be secured close to the necklace end and bead.

To use a cupped necklace end
1 Thread the strand(s) through the hole at the bottom of the necklace end cup.
2 Crush a crimp with flat-nose pliers or tie a knot in the thread.
3 Hook the metal tail of the necklace end onto a clasp and loop it back on itself. For the second end, use pliers to crimp or to move and tighten the knot as close as possible to the necklace end.

Opening and closing jump rings

It is best to open and close a jump ring using two pairs of pliers.
1 Locate the split in the ring where the two ends meet. Holding each side with the two pairs of pliers, pull

one side towards you and push the other side away from you.

2 Connect the jump ring and repeat Step 2 in reverse. This way you open and close the jump ring without deforming the shape.

Making a headpin loop

Headpins are used to hang beads and for making pendants. They are also especially useful for making earrings.
1 Hold the headpin with round-nose pliers, leaving a tail at the top of at least 1.5 cm (½ in). Twist your hand and the pliers to bend the headpin so that, looking straight on, it looks like 10 to 6 on a clock face. Here you'll notice that one jaw is on top. Smooth the tail back around the top jaw so that the tail is pointing down the same way as the main body.

2 Release your grip on the pin with the pliers and rotate until one jaw is above and one is inside the part-made loop. Continue to smooth the tail completely around the jaw in the middle of the loop so it crosses the main body of the pin. Remove the headpin from the pliers.

3 Holding onto the tail – the piece you are cutting off – rest the wire cutters on the shoulder formed in Step 1. Snip off the tail with the wire cutters.

Couching beads onto fabric

1 You will need two sharp needles on two separate lengths of thread. Tie a knot in the first length of thread and bring up through the fabric where you want the beadwork to begin. Pick up the beads with the needle. Bring the second needle and thread up between the first and second beads.

2 With the second needle and thread, start sewing down every third or fourth bead by passing the needle over the beads.

3 Continue to the end and secure both threads neatly to finish.

Beaded backstitch

1 Knot the end of a piece of thread and, using a sharp beading needle, bring the needle up through the fabric. Place a bead on the needle and push down to the fabric.

2 Make a backstitch by bringing the point of the needle up where you want the next bead to be. Add a bead and repeat the backstitch.

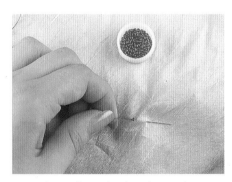

3 You can place the beads as close or far apart as you wish. This stitch can be used with all beads from seed to bugles for various effects.

Fringing

1 Thread a sharp beading needle with plenty of thread and attach firmly to the fabric with a few running stitches. Thread on the required number or beads to make the fringe the correct length.

2 Thread a small round bead onto the end of the fringe (this acts as the "turning bead") and pass the needle back up through the fringe.

3 Add a stitch at the top and then make a running stitch along the fabric to where you want to position the next fringe. Repeat from Step 1.

Peyote stitch

Peyote stitch is very versatile and can be used to make a whole range of items, such as the choker on pages 42-45. Peyote stitch can be created as even or odd count and flat or in a tube. These instructions are for flat, even-count peyote.

1 Thread a sharp beading needle with a length of Nymo. Place a stopper bead on the end of the thread by looping back through the bead. This stops your beads from falling off the end of the thread and is removed when the project is finished. It is best to use a different coloured bead to avoid confusion. Using the needle to pick them up, thread on an even number of beads. Peyote stitch is best worked in two colours (A and B) so that you can see the rows building up. You are threading away from the stopper.

2 For the second row, pick up a bead – the same colour as the last bead on the first row (A) – and pass the needle back through the next-to-last bead. Pick up another bead in the same colour, miss a bead and pass the needle through the next bead. Continue all the way down the end of the row, missing every other bead. You should now be working back towards the stopper bead. Add a third row by picking up a bead (B),

missing the next bead along and passing the needle once more through the odd-numbered bead. Repeat all the way down the row.

3 For the fourth row, pick up a bead (A) and pass the needle through the bead that sticks out. Repeat up the row, making sure the tension is firm.

Adding extra thread

Adding extra thread is only necessary where you will be using a particularly large amount of thread, such as with peyote stitch. For all other projects you should start with enough thread.

1 Leave a tail of the first thread and thread the needle with the second thread. Starting a little way back through the weaving, thread the needle through the pattern a second time, ensuring that you can still see the tail – you can snip this off later.

2 Work your way through the last few beads in the pattern to get to the point you stopped at. Pull on the new thread to see if there is enough tension holding it in the weave. If not, pull the thread through and start again a little further back.

Making a spiral rope

Spiral rope is a form of beadweaving which creates a chain which can be made to any length. It is ideal for making necklaces and bracelets.

1 Thread a sharp beading needle with a length of Nymo. Place a stopper bead (to stop your bead falling off) on the end of the thread by looping back through the bead. Thread on four size 10 seed beads for the core, then three in a contrasting colour. Thread the needle back up through the four core beads.

2 Thread on one core bead and three outsiders – in the contrasting colour. Pass the needle up through the top four core beads, leaving out the bottom one.

3 Repeat Step 2, making sure the outside beads always lie either to the right or the left of the previous row, otherwise it the rope will not "spiral" properly.

Using a bead loom

Bead loom weaving is a quick and easy way of weaving beads to make a flat strip. The beads are arranged in straight rows so the design can be worked out on a grid in advance. If you want to create your own designs use the grid on page 78.

1 Count the number of beads across the design and add one – this will be the number of warp thread. Measure out the number of threads you are using to your required length with an additional 30 cm (1 ft) on each. You will need one more thread than the number of beads per row. Knot them together at one end. Hook the knot over the nail (anchor) at one end of the loom. Wrap the thread round the spool and tighten the nut.

2 Separate the threads out on the spring so that each is in a separate groove, next to the previous one.

3 Tie the other ends of the thread together and repeat the process on the other end of the loom. Take care to make sure the threads do not cross over and that they are held taut. These are the warp threads.
4 When you have finished the weaving, release one end of your work at a time. Start by pairing up the threads and tying a simple knot in each pair. Pull the knot so it moves down the two strands and sits next to the bead, this keeps the tension. If you have an odd number of threads then tie three strands together.
5 Thread all strands through beads using a flexible beading needle, to the required length, before adding a clasp, or you can plait the strands together before adding a clasp. Repeat at the other side of your work.

Stretchy crystal bracelet

HANA GLOVER

Crystal beads make fantastic sparkly bracelets, and when threaded onto elastic no clasp is needed. I am always experimenting to find new ways to use crystal cubes – they're such a fascinating shape! This bracelet is stunning but very easy to make.

"As well as looking good, the seed beads on either side protect the elastic from the edges of the cubes, which can be sharp."

You will need

Materials

- 60 x 4 mm crystal AB faceted beads
- 1.5 m (5 ft) length of 0.5 mm (25 SWG) Stretch Magic elastic
- 60 x size 8 or 9 crystal AB seed beads
- 30 x 4 mm fuchsia crystal cubes
- 2 tubular crimps

Tools

- Masking tape (optional)
- Scissors
- Flat-nose pliers

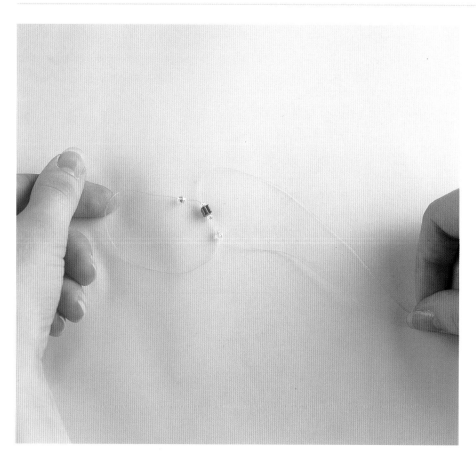

1 Thread two 4 mm crystal AB beads onto 1.5 m (5 ft) of Stretch Magic elastic. Now thread on one crystal seed bead, one crystal cube and another seed bead. Take the other end of the elastic and thread it back through the seed bead, cube and seed bead group in the opposite direction. Pull the ends of the elastic to move the beads down towards the bottom of the thread, leaving a 10 cm (4 in) loop. The loop can be taped to the work surface to keep it in place.

★☆☆ **Skill level** · 🕐 **1–2 hours**

2 Thread another 4 mm AB bead onto each end of the elastic. As before, thread a seed, a cube then another seed onto one end of the elastic and thread the other end back through in the opposite direction. Pull the ends of the elastic to move the beads down to join the first set.

3 Continue adding groups of 4 mm AB, seed, cube and seed in the same fashion until the bracelet has approximately 28 cube beads.

4 Thread a tubular crimp onto each end of the elastic. Cut the tail loop of elastic formed in Step 1 in two. Thread each new end through the crimp on the other end of the bracelet (take care to thread through the corresponding crimp bead so the bracelet doesn't have a twist in it.

5 Pull the ends of the elastic tight and crush the crimp bead with a pair of flat-nose pliers. Repeat on the other side and trim the excess elastic.

Helpful hint
Tubular crimps are smooth and less likely to shear the elastic when crushed.

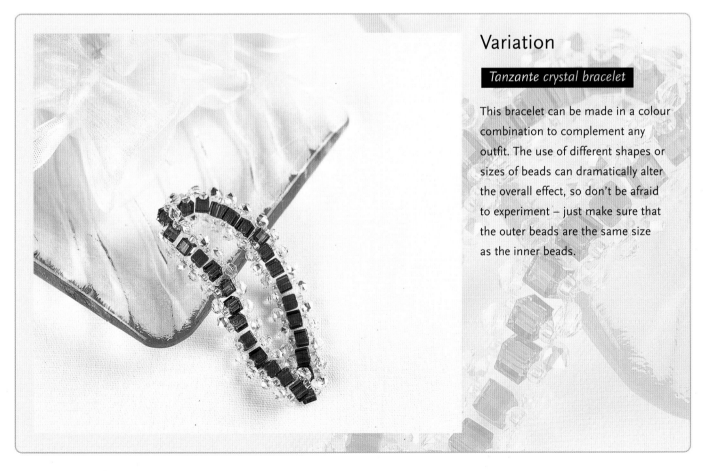

Variation

Tanzante crystal bracelet

This bracelet can be made in a colour combination to complement any outfit. The use of different shapes or sizes of beads can dramatically alter the overall effect, so don't be afraid to experiment – just make sure that the outer beads are the same size as the inner beads.

Semiprecious stone earrings

ROBIN BELLINGHAM

Semiprecious stone chips, or tumblechips, are great beads to use because their irregular shape gives the finished project an individuality that cannot be exactly reproduced. These earrings feature mother-of-pearl, which is believed to promote wealth, and rose quartz, believed to promote love.

"These simple earrings are great for beginners and make unique gifts, because no two pairs will be the same."

You will need

Materials

- 8 x 15 cm (6 in) lengths of 0.6 mm (22 SWG) silver-plated wire (more if required)
- Rose quartz and mother-of-pearl semiprecious tumblechips (you will need about 12 of each colour)
- 2 sterling-silver fishhooks

Tools

- Round-nose pliers
- Flat-nose pliers
- Wire cutters

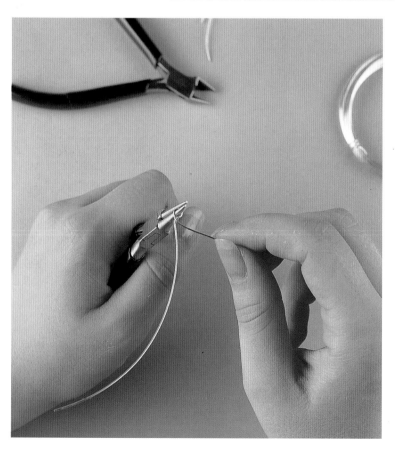

1 Take one 15 cm (6 in) length of 0.6 mm (22 SWG) wire. Grip the wire with round-nose pliers about 5 cm (2 in) from one end. The wire is now divided into two sections – a long stem and a shorter tail. Holding the tail end, twist your hand and the pliers to start bending the wire into a loop around the top jaw of the pliers. Using your free thumb, continue smoothing the tail around the top jaw of the pliers until it is pointing the same way as the stem. Release your grip with the pliers but do not remove them. Rotate the pliers until you have one jaw above the loop. Now finish the loop by moving the tail all of the way around the plier jaw so it crosses the stem.

★☆☆ **Skill level**   🕐 **1 hour**   **Techniques:** *Making a headpin loop p.14*

2 Do not cut the tail off. Instead hold the loop between the jaws of a pair of flat-nose pliers where the wire crosses itself. Ensure the tail of the loop is above the stem. Holding the very end of the tail of wire, pull and wrap it under and around the stem two or three times.

3 Trim what is left of the tail as close to the stem as possible and tuck in and crimp the remaining tail with the pliers. Squash the first coil, the one next to the loop, a little so that it grips the stem. Now use wire cutters to cut off the loop as close to the bottom coil as possible. This will stop the beads falling off.

4 Thread on as many rose quartz tumblechips as you like. Once you have the desired length, leave at least 6 cm (2½ in) at the top to recreate the same coil effect as the bottom. Leave a small gap between the top tumblechip and the start of the loop.

5 Follow Steps 1–2 to make the top loop and coil. Do not cut off the loop, as this will be used to connect the earring pin to the fishhook. Trim and crimp in the tail of the coil to neaten.

6 Make a second pin using mother-of-pearl tumblechips, this time using a few more beads to make a slightly longer pin. Use round-nose pliers to twist open the loop on a silver fishhook and thread each pin through it. Twist close the fishhook loop and repeat all the steps to make the second of the pair.

Helpful hint
For the best effect, vary the lengths of the pins when you have more than one pin on each fishhook.

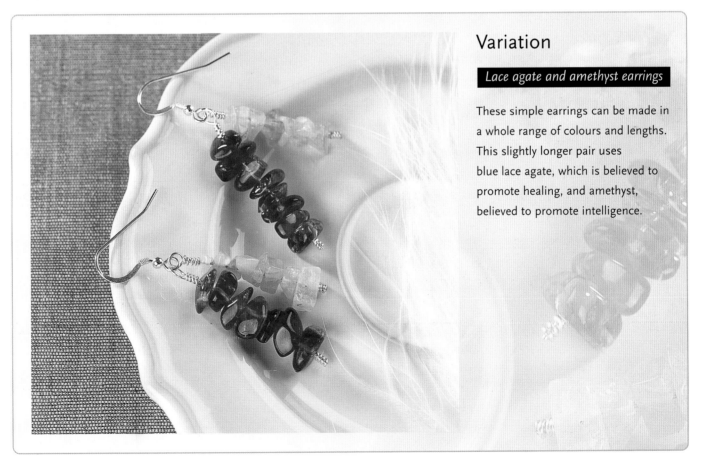

Variation

Lace agate and amethyst earrings

These simple earrings can be made in a whole range of colours and lengths. This slightly longer pair uses blue lace agate, which is believed to promote healing, and amethyst, believed to promote intelligence.

Sunset crystal necklace

ROBIN BELLINGHAM

Most beading projects are designed on symmetrical patterns. Even when a random design is desired the beader will generally fall into creating a pattern. The beads on this necklace may follow a roughly measured repetition, but the project uses a random mix of colours and is a beautifully simple way of using up spare crystals and seed beads.

"Don't be tempted to use superglue, it is hard to control and if it gets on the beads it gives them a frosty white coating."

You will need

Materials

- 4 lengths of clear monofilament: 38 cm (15 in); 40 cm (16 in); 43 cm (17 in); and 45 cm (18 in)
- 2 gold-plated necklace ends
- 2 crimps
- a selection of 4 mm crystal beads in oranges, reds and golds (you will need about 30 in total)
- a selection of silver-lined seed beads, sizes 10 and 11, in topaz AB, orange AB, gold, orange and red (you will need about 80 in total)
- Clear bead glue
- Gold-plated trigger clasp
- 4 mm (¼ in) gold-plated jump ring

Tools

- Scissors
- Flat-nose pliers
- Small container

1 Thread all four strands of clear monofilament through a necklace end and then a crimp. At the end of the threads, crush the crimp bead against the threads with flat-nose pliers and trim away any excess. Close the necklace end over the crimp with the pliers.

2 Pour all the beads into a small container to help you pick out the beads at random. Each bead is secured onto an individual thread with a very small amount of glue. Put a small blob of glue on the strand where you want the first bead to sit, then move the bead onto the glue.

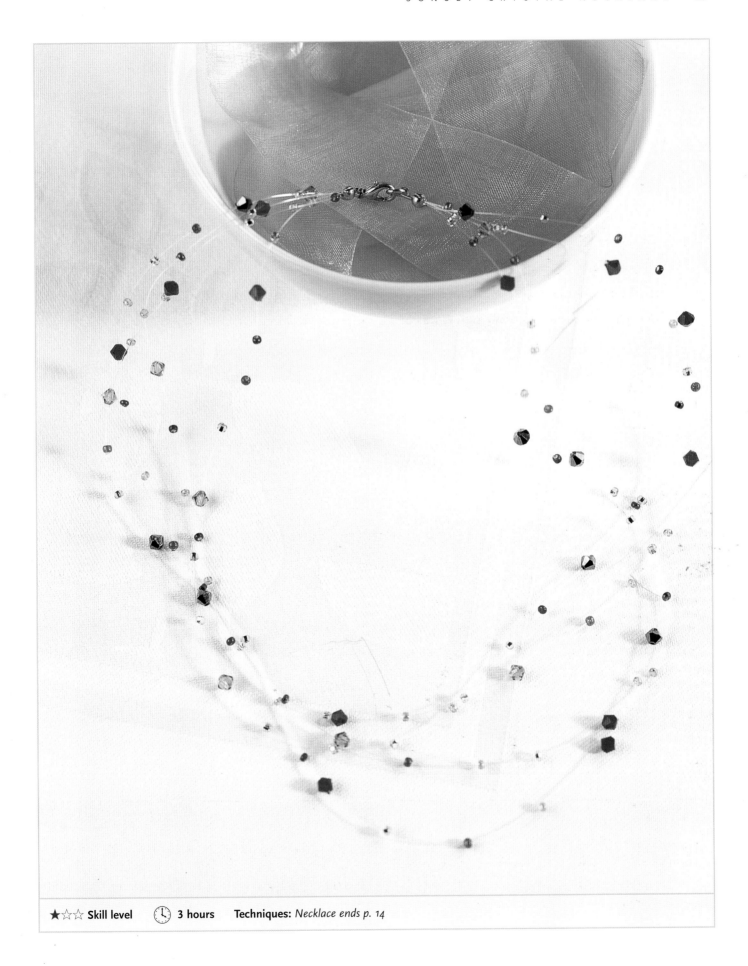

★☆☆ **Skill level**   🕐 **3 hours**   **Techniques:** *Necklace ends p. 14*

3 Working on one thread at a time, continue adding more beads picked out at random. Space the beads approximately 1.5–2 cm (½–1 in) apart. The spacing doesn't have to be exact as the scattered effect adds to the look and texture of the necklace.

Helpful hint
You may find it easier to control the amount of glue you use if you dispense it with a needle or headpin.

4 When each of the strands has been decorated with the desired number of beads, leave the glue to dry. Then thread all the strands through a necklace end and another crimp. Ensure the threads aren't twisted before you crush the crimp with pliers.

5 Close the necklace end over the crimp, hook the metal tail of the necklace end onto a gold-plated trigger clasp and loop it back on itself to close. Attach a jump ring to the other necklace end in the same way.

Helpful hint
If you have enough time, it is easier to work if you leave each strand to dry before starting on the next.

Variation

Silver and pink combination

This style of necklace will work in any colourway, just remember to alter the colour of the clasp you use to suit the shade of the beads. Use gold-plated with warm colours and silver-plated with cool colours.

Beaded hair comb

JEMA HEWITT

Whether your hair is long or short, this beaded comb is sure to show it off to its full potential. The thick cluster of sparkle is just the thing to wear with a simple party dress at a formal dinner party, and is so easy to make you could create one for every occasion. This project uses basic manipulation of wire and a variety of beads to create a very rich texture.

"In pastel shades the comb would look wonderful as a bridesmaid's accessory."

You will need

Materials

- 2 m (80 in) length of 0.4 mm (27 SWG) silver-plated wire
- 18 x 4 mm silver-coloured pearl beads
- 3 x 5 mm dark red crystal beads
- 18 x 4 mm green fire polish beads
- Plain hair comb
- Assortment of size 10 seed beads and crystal beads up to 8 mm in various green colours

Tools

- Tape measure
- Wire cutters

1 Start by making the flowers. Cut 15 cm (6 in) of wire and thread on six 4 mm silver pearl beads. Push them halfway down the wire and twist the wire around until the beads form a circle. Twist the wire twice to hold the beads in place.

2 Separate the two end wires and thread a 5 mm dark red crystal bead on one strand. Push one wire to the front and one to the back of the pearl flower and position the crystal in the centre of the pearl flower. Twist the two wire strands together to hold the crystal in place. Make three flowers in the same way.

3 To make the leaves, thread nine 4 mm fire polish beads onto a 10 cm (4 in) length of wire. Push them to the middle of the wire. Loop the wire round to make a leaf shape and twist the ends of the wire all the way down. Make two leaves. Twist together the wire stem of one leaf and one flower. Twist together the second leaf and the remaining two flowers. Bend the wires at a 45 degree angle, 1 cm ($3/8$ in) from the heads. This is so that the flowers and leaves stand upright when you come to wrap them round the comb.

4 Cut 50 cm (20 in) of wire and attach to the comb at the left end by firmly wrapping round three times. Hold one of the flower bunches along the length of the comb so the flower heads stand upright on the left. Wrap the long piece of wire around twice, very tightly, to begin securing.

5 Thread a random selection of beads onto the end of the wire and start wrapping the beaded wire round the comb, working down from left to right. When you have covered about 2 cm ($3/4$ in) add the next flower bunch. Continue wrapping the beaded wire, adding more beads as necessary.

6 At the end of the comb, fasten by wrapping unbeaded wire tightly three times along the whole length of the comb. Trim the wire and tweak the flowers and leaves until they make a pleasing arrangement.

Helpful hint

For a vintage look, use a metal comb instead of an acrylic one. It will also last longer.

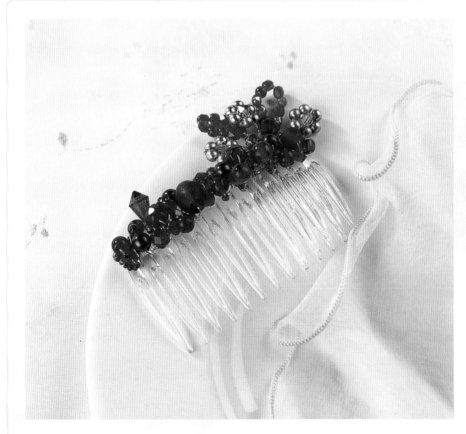

Variation

Red and gold alternative

These combs are a wonderful way to display individual special beads, so use the same techniques to make variations on the theme, experimenting with different colours.

Turquoise charm bracelet

JEMA HEWITT

This simple bracelet is a perfect way to display a selection of precious art beads, homemade beads, pendants and charms. I fell in love with the turquoise rabbit and just had to show him off, so I chose greens and blues with lapis lazuli tumblechips to complement it. This project is also a good way to use up leftover 8 mm beads. The more interesting a mix of bead types the better the end effect.

"Bracelets with personalized charms make wonderful presents."

You will need

Materials

- 6 charms, pendants or art beads
- 6 sterling-silver jump rings or headpins
- A few assorted size 10 seed beads
- 2 sterling-silver necklace ends
- 15 cm (6 in) length of 0.4 mm (27 SWG) tigertail
- 2 silver crimps
- Superglue (optional)
- 14 x 8 mm round beads, a mix of plain and faceted glass and crystal
- 13 large tumblechips
- Sterling-silver clasp

Tools

- 2 pairs of flat-nose pliers
- Round-nose pliers
- Wire cutters

1 First make the charms and beads ready to dangle. If a charm or pendant has a hole at the top, a jump ring can be attached and closed. Choose a jump ring big enough to leave a gap at the top for the bracelet cord. Twist the ring with two pairs of pliers to open, insert through the pendant hole and twist back again to close.

Helpful hint
If you have a brittle crystal charm, use a triangular clamp instead.

2 If the hole goes from the top to the bottom of the bead, place it on a headpin with a seed bead or two, top and bottom, so the charm doesn't fall off. Make a loop at the top of the headpin with round-nose pliers. To do this, curve the wire around the pliers leaving a tail. Grip the loop flat in flat-nose pliers and wrap the wire around the stem a few times to finish. Trim any spare wire with wire cutters.

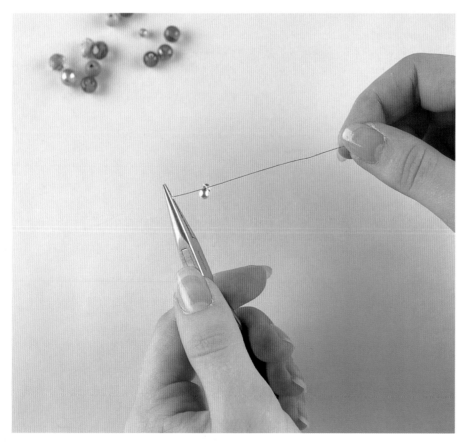

3 Cut a 15 cm (6 in) length of tigertail and thread on a necklace end and then a crimp. Push to the end of the tigertail and crush the crimp with the flat-nose pliers. Make sure it is completely secure, then close up the necklace end very gently over the crimp with the pliers. For extra security you could put a dab of superglue on the crimp too.

Helpful hint
Tigertail is very strong but you could use beading thread instead.

4 Place the 8 mm round beads and tumblechips in front of you in a pleasing but random arrangement. Thread on a bead, a tumblechip, another bead, a tumblechip and a charm. Repeat the pattern until you have used all the beads and charms.

5 Attach the final necklace end as before and trim any excess tigertail with wire cutters. Add a silver clasp, attaching each end to the necklace ends by closing the loops with round-nose pliers.

Variation

Charm ideas

Always keep an eye out for special beads to use as charms, or try making your own from polymer clay.

Victorian drop necklace

HANA GLOVER

This elegant project was inspired by the beautiful Victorian jet necklaces and collars that became popular after Queen Victoria went into mourning following the death of her beloved husband Albert, although I have chosen pretty, light colours for this project. It would look effective in almost any colour combination.

"A jet necklace, such as the variation on page 41, would traditionally be made from the famous Whitby jet."

You will need

Materials
- 2 m (6½ ft) length of 0.6 mm (23 SWG) lilac beading thread
- 2 silver necklace ends
- 15 g size 7 crystal AB seed beads
- 12 x 4 mm violet bicone beads
- 8 x 6 mm violet bicone drop beads
- Superglue (optional)
- Triangular clamp
- Large crystal AB drop pendant

- Necklace tag
- Trigger clasp

Tools
- Scissors
- Flexible beading needle (optional)
- Flat-nose pliers

1 Cut two 75 cm (30 in) lengths of beading thread. Push both ends through a necklace end, knot together and close the necklace end over the knot with flat-nose pliers. Thread 11 size 7 seed beads onto one thread and 15 onto the other. Add a 4 mm bicone bead, threading it through both threads, and pull tight. The lower thread will now form a loop underneath the first one.

2 Thread 20 size 7 seed beads onto the lower thread. On the top one add six size 7 seed beads, one 6 mm bicone drop bead then another six size 7 seed beads. Then thread a 4 mm bicone onto both threads. This forms the second loop.

Helpful hint
If you find it difficult to thread the beads, use a flexible beading needle or apply superglue to the ends of the thread to stiffen them.

3 Add 25 size 7 seed beads onto the lower thread. Thread eight size 7, one 6 mm bicone drop and eight size 7 seeds onto the top thread, then pass both threads through a 4 mm bicone bead. Thread 30 size 7 seeds onto the lower thread. Onto the top thread add ten size 7 seeds, one 6 mm bicone and ten size 7 seeds, then thread both ends through a 4 mm bicone. To the lower thread add 15 size 7 seeds, a 4 mm bicone and 15 size 7 seeds. On the top thread add 12 size 7 seeds, one 6 mm bicone drop and 12 size 7 seeds. Then thread both ends through a 4 mm bicone bead.

4 Attach a triangular clamp to a large crystal AB drop pendant. Thread both threads through the clamp. Add another 4 mm bicone bead, then continue making loops mirroring the other side of the necklace (following the instructions in the opposite direction to make loops that decrease in size).

5 When all the loops have been made add a necklace end with flat-nose pliers. Hook the metal tail of the neckace end through a necklace tag and close the loop with flat-nose pliers. Attach a trigger clasp to the other necklace end in the same way.

Variation

Traditional drop necklace

This version shows how the traditional necklaces looked. It makes a very elegant eveningwear accessory for formal events.

Candy stripe bead choker

ROBIN BELLINGHAM

Peyote stitch is one of many beadweaving stitches, and an easy stitch to master. When using Delica beads there are no gaps between the beads, each bead will fit snugly with its neighbour, leaving a very tidy project. In this project I have used even-count peyote stitch, and you can see the pattern grow very quickly.

"A small tube of peyote stitch beadweaving looks modern and dramatic on a plain necklace choker."

You will need

Materials

- 1 m (3 ft) length of purple Nymo D or Silamide thread
- 5 g DB610 silver-lined violet size 11 Delicas (dark Delica bead)
- 5 g DB041 silver-lined crystal size 11 Delicas (light Delica bead)
- Necklace choker with screw-off bead or similar necklace thread

Tools

- Masking tape
- Size 10 beading needle

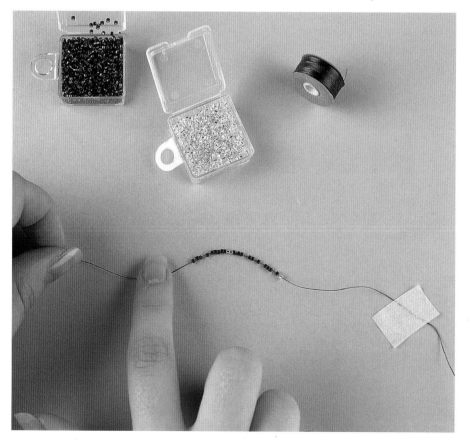

1 Start by taping the Nymo D or Silamide thread to your work surface, about 10 cm (4 in) from one end. Thread the beads from the other end, with the first bead stopping about about 10 cm (4 in) from the tape. Thread on 22 beads in this order: 1 light, 10 dark, 2 light, 9 dark. Thread a beading needle onto the end of the thread.

Helpful hint
Use beeswax or a commercial thread conditioner on the thread to help to stop it tangling.

★★☆ **Skill level** 🕐 **2 hours** **Techniques:** *Peyote stitch p. 16*

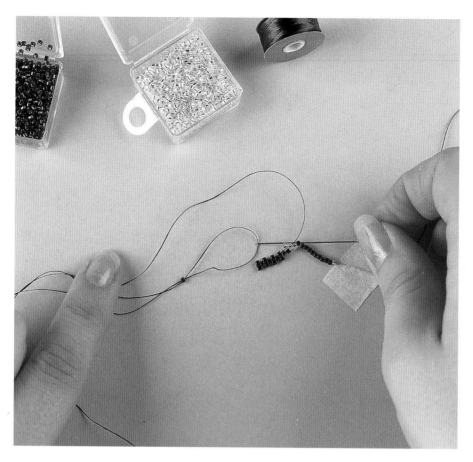

2   Add one dark bead (bead 23), then thread the needle through bead 21, missing bead 22, working towards the tape. Pull the thread through until beads 22 and 23 are side by side. Add a second dark bead, miss one bead and thread through bead 19. Pull the thread and bead 19 will push bead 20 and the dark bead you have just added side by side. A pattern will start developing. Each time you add a bead, miss out the next bead on the original 22 beads and thread through the next one in line. You will only be threading through the odd-numbered beads. The fifth bead added when threading back towards the tape should be a light bead. Add four more dark beads as above; the last bead on this row should be a light bead.

3   You will notice a pattern of beads that stick out from the main body of beads. Thread through each of these beads after you have added each of the following beads in succession. **Row 4:** (working away from the tape) add 1 dark (thread through), add 1 light (thread through), add 1 dark (thread through), add 1 dark (thread through), add 1 dark (thread through), add 1 dark (thread through), add 1 dark (thread through), add 1 light (thread through), add 1 dark (thread through), add 1 dark (thread through), add 1 dark (thread through). **Row 5:** (working towards the tape) 3 dark, 1 light, 5 dark, 1 light, 1 dark. **Row 6:** (working away from the tape) 2 dark, 1 light, 5 dark, 1 light, 2 dark. **Row 7:** (working towards the tape) 2 dark, 1 light, 5 dark, 1 light, 2 dark. **Row 8:** (working away from the tape) 3 dark, 1 light, 5 dark, 1 light, 1 dark. **Row 9:** (working towards the tape) 1 dark, 1 light, 5 dark, 1 light, 3 dark. **Row 10:** (working away from the tape) 4 dark, 1 light, 5 dark, 1 light. **Row 11:** (working towards the tape) 1 light, 4 dark, 1 light, 5 dark. **Row 12:** (working away from the tape) 5 dark, 1 light, 5 dark.

4 Once you have completed these 12 rows, you should be in the position to sew the two long edges together. If you bring both edges together you will find that they sit snugly. Sew through each edge bead, sewing from one bead through the next bead until you have a complete tube. Hide the tail of thread by weaving back through the pattern until you lose the tail or you are satisfied that you can cut it off. Repeat for the other tail, at the beginning of the peyote stitch.

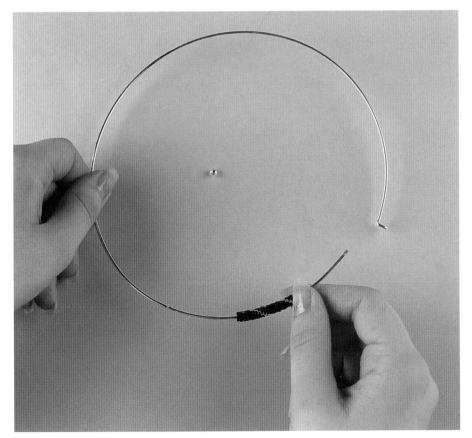

5 Unscrew the bead tip from the necklace choker and thread on the peyote-stitch tube. Gently push it round to the front of the choker and replace the bead tip.

Helpful hint
You could also continue the peyote-stitch pattern to make a longer length tube.

Embroidered bag

JEMA HEWITT

Once you have learned the techniques for sewing beads onto fabric you just won't be able to stop. In Elizabethan times clothes were embroidered with real pearls and precious gems. In the 1920s beads were used all over fine fabrics to add weight and texture. Today, richly beaded clothing has enjoyed a renewed popularity.

"This gorgeous beaded purse uses a variety of techniques as inspiration and the design can be placed on any surface, such as the edge of a shawl or as decoration on a blouse or bodice."

You will need

Materials

- A ready-made purse or bag
- Tailor's chalk pencil, in a shade close to the bag colour, or tailor's carbon paper and wheel
- Sewing thread
- Approximately 40 size 10 seed beads
- Approximately 15 x 4 mm crystal beads
- Approximately 80 bugle beads

Tools

- Size 10 beading needle

1 Make sure the bag you have chosen does not have the material tightly stretched over it as this will make embroidery very difficult. The best type is a gathered pouch or "Dorothy" bag.

2 Photocopy the template on page 78, enlarging if necessary. Draw on the design freehand with a tailor's pencil, using the photocopy as a guide, or use tailor's carbon paper and wheel to trace the main elements of the design. You do not need to transfer every single bead placement, just the main parts so the finished piece will all be in proportion.

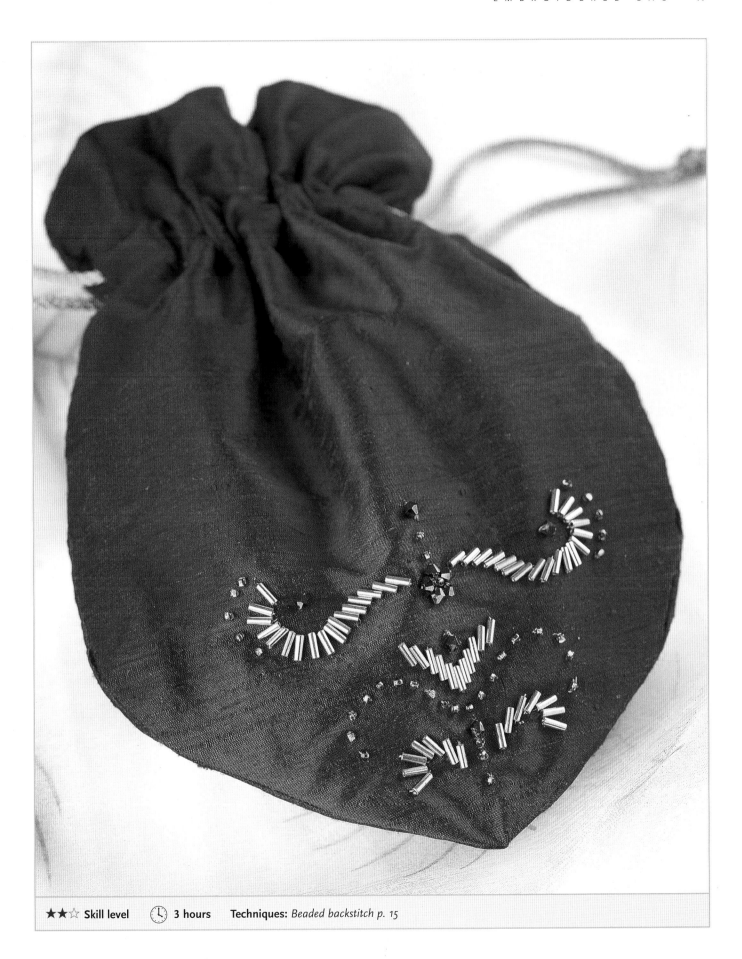

★★☆ **Skill level**   🕐 **3 hours**   **Techniques:** *Beaded backstitch p. 15*

3 Thread the needle and tie a knot in the end of the thread. Bring the needle up through the fabric, starting in the centre of the design, and sew on a central seed bead and the five crystals using beaded backstitch (see page 15). Next attach the bugle beads one by one in a swirl on either side of the cluster. Be careful not to catch in the lining when sewing, and if you have to move the thread across a large distance under the work, don't pull it too tight, then take a little stitch to hold it before starting the next row of beads. You may find it easier to place the bag on your hand when sewing, rather than on the table.

4 Sew on all the other bugle beads in the same way. Next attach the crystal beads firmly. Stitch through them each a couple of times as these heavier beads will wear the thread more quickly.

Helpful hint
If you are embroidering a homesewn item, it is often easier to do the beadwork embellishment before making up the item.

5 Finally attach the seed beads into place using beaded backstitch (see page 15). If you need to add thread, finish off by stitching over and over in an inconspicuous place and snip the tail close to the fabric. Start new thread by stitching over and over under the first bead to be sewn on. Don't be afraid to unpick and start again if a bead isn't quite where you want it, but also be patient and try to judge the overall effect before deciding if the bead is really noticeably wrong.

Variation

Your own design

Designing your own embroidery is very rewarding; take inspiration from patterns and motifs on wallpaper, stationery and even vases. Each era in history has its own distinct style and books on historical decoration are invaluable. Think about which type of bead to use where. Dense areas of seed beads, for example, can be used to great effect, as can sequins.

Bead loom bracelet

HANA GLOVER

Native American Indian beadwork was traditionally made with materials such as shell, bone and turquoise. When the Americas were colonized, European beads such as glass pony beads and seed beads were introduced. These were originally only available in a small number of opaque colours.

"This design is inspired by the traditional colours and the geometric patterns favoured by some tribes. I have used a toggle clasp to fasten the bracelet as they are much easier to do up single-handed."

You will need

Materials

- Strong sewing thread, in a colour to match the beads
- Size 10 seed beads in opaque blue, opaque red, opaque light blue and opaque turquoise (approximately 120 of each colour)
- Glue
- 2 necklace ends
- Toggle clasp

Tools

- Tape measure
- Bead loom
- Flat-nose pliers
- Size 10 beading needle
- Flexible beading needle

1 Measure out eight 50 cm (20 in) lengths of thread. Knot them together at one end, Hook the knot over the nail (anchor) at one end of a bead loom. Wrap the thread round the spool and tighten the nut. Separate the threads out on the spring so that each thread is in a separate groove, next to the previous one. Tie the other end of the thread and repeat the process on the other end of the loom. Take care to make sure the threads do not cross over each other and they are held taut. These are the warp threads.

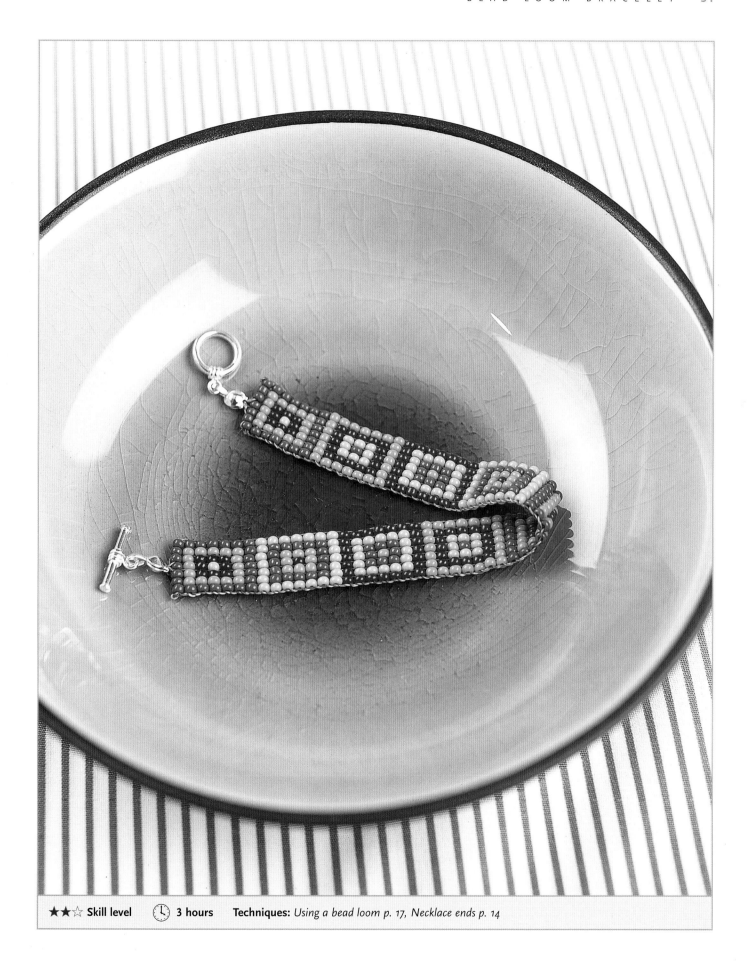

★★☆ **Skill level** 🕐 **3 hours** **Techniques:** *Using a bead loom p. 17, Necklace ends p. 14*

Thread another 1.5 m (5 ft) of thread onto a beading needle. Knot the thread onto the furthest left warp thread at the bottom of the loom, next to the spring, leaving a 10 cm (4 in) tail. This is the weft thread. Thread seven blue seed beads onto the needle. Place the needle underneath the warp threads, push the beads up so that one bead sits between each of the warp threads. Then pull the needle and thread through the beads, using your finger to hold the beads in position. To secure the beads in place, bring the needle to the front of the loom and thread it back through the beads in the opposite direction. Pull the thread tight and straighten out the line.

Continue adding the beads row by row, following the pattern above, until the bracelet is the desired length. To make a necklace, book mark, belt, etc, follow the above instructions but alter the length of the warp threads. These should be the length of the desired finished item plus 40 cm (16 in).

Thread on one blue, five turquoise, and one blue bead. Hold the needle underneath the warp threads with the beads spaced one between each thread. As before, pull the needle and thread through the beads underneath the warp threads, then back through them in the opposite direction on top of the warp threads. Pull tight and straighten the beads.

5 To make the item longer than the loom, loosen the nuts and gently lift the work off the springs. Move it down the loom to where there is enough space to continue the work. Tighten the nuts and continue beading as before.

6 When the bracelet is complete, loosen the nuts and remove it from the loom. Knot the warp threads in adjacent pairs, except the last knot, which will also include the weft thread. Repeat at the other end of the bracelet.

7 Thread the two left-hand knotted threads onto a flexible beading needle. Thread through the first three seed beads, from the left-hand side, towards the centre of the bracelet. Repeat with the right-hand threads so that all the threads are in the centre. Now use the flexible beading needle to thread all the strands through a necklace end. Knot the threads together and put a spot of glue on the knot. Then close a necklace end over it with flat-nose pliers. Hook on one end of a toggle clasp and close the loop of the necklace end by squeezing gently with a pair of flat-nose pliers. Repeat on the other end of the bracelet.

Beaded cushion tassel

JEMA HEWITT

I adore tassels; there is something about them that transforms the most mundane item into something really sophisticated. The flappers of the 1920s knew this and wore them on coats, dresses, bags – even as necklaces! This cushion cover is elevated to a wonderful chic accessory that any sofa would be proud to wear.

"If cushions aren't your thing, why not add a tassel to a light pull, a purse or the end of your sewing scissors?"

You will need

Materials
- Very fine, silky thread, machine embroidery cotton is good
- 15 x 10 cm (6 x 4 in) rectangle of card
- Strong buttonhole thread, in the same colour as the embroidery thread
- 15 g size 10 seed beads in two contrasting colours
- 1 m (3 ft) length of gold Nymo D or Silamide thread

- Ready-made cushion cover
- Glue (optional)

Tools
- Tape measure
- Scissors
- Size 10 beading needle
- Sewing needle

1 To make the basic tassel, wrap fine embroidery thread around the longest part of a cardboard rectangle. About 200 wraps of the finest thread is enough, less if you use thicker cotton. If you intend to make more than one tassel, count how many wraps you have done so each tassel has the same plumpness.

2 Cut 20 cm (8 in) of buttonhole thread and tuck it between the threads and cardboard. Pull the buttonhole thread to the top edge of the cardboard and tie a square or reef knot very tightly to bind the embroidery threads together. Don't trim the long buttonhole threads just yet.

★★☆ **Skill level**   🕐 **3 hours**   **Techniques:** *Peyote stitch p. 16*

3 Snip through the bottom loops of the threads at the edge of the cardboard, holding the top part of the tassel in one hand. Cut a length of the fine embroidery thread and wrap it tightly around the top 1 cm (½ in) of the tassel, creating a wrapped head. Tie the ends in a square or reef knot and trim. Trim the bottom edge evenly as well.

Helpful hint
Use small, very sharp scissors to trim the tassel.

4 Make a square of peyote stitch by attaching a stopper bead to about 1 m (3 ft) of Nymo D or Silamide thread. Loop the thread and needle back through a seed bead to stop it moving. Thread on 12 alternately coloured seed beads. Work peyote stitches by picking up a bead of the same colour as the last threaded on and pass the needle back down through the bead of opposite colour next to it. Work your way down the row, adding a bead of one colour but passing the needle through the beads of the opposite colour (see page 16).

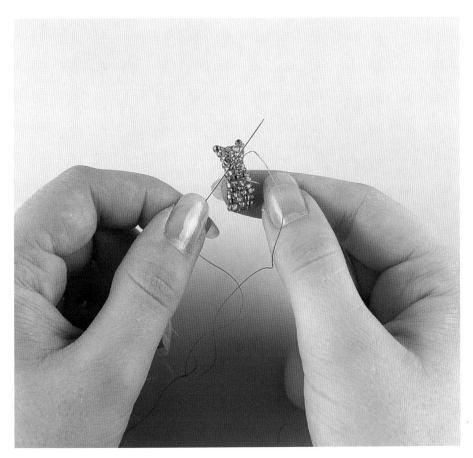

5 Keep the tension firm and when you have about eight beads at top and bottom of the piece, check the size by wrapping it around the tassel head, it should fit nice and tightly. If it is too small add more rows until it is a comfortable fit. Make sure the beads sticking out on each side are of opposite colours. Sew together the two long edges, threading the needle through one bead on each side. Finish the thread off by weaving through the beads.

6 Slip the beaded head over the silk tassel, if you want to make it very firm you could either glue it into place or sew through a few times.

7 Attach the tassel to the cushion cover using the two long buttonhole threads and a sharp sewing needle. Just sew over and over very neatly and trim the excess thread. Sew the tassels fairly close to the cushion but not so tight that they don't lie properly.

Flower choker card

HANA GLOVER

Handmade cards make wonderful presents with a personal touch. Combining them with an item of jewellery makes the perfect gift, which will be treasured. This design is inspired by French beaded flowers, which are thought to date back to the 15th century.

"French beaded flowers can be very beautiful but are time-consuming and complicated to make. This design is much quicker and makes a flatter piece, ideal for mounting on ribbon or card."

You will need

Materials

- 1 m (3 ft) length of 0.3 mm (30 SWG) clear monofilament
- 12 size 7 seed beads
- 15 g size 10 transparent blue seed beads
- 15 g size 10 silver-lined blue seed beads
- 1 x 8 mm faceted blue bead
- 50 cm (20 in) length of wired fabric ribbon (reasonably sturdy to hold weight of flower)
- Glue
- Iron-on Velcro

- Sewing thread
- Coordinating card and envelope
- Double-sided tape (optional)

Tools

- Tape measure
- Scissors
- Iron
- Sewing needle

1 To make the flower, thread 12 size 7 seed beads onto the monofilament. Pass the thread through all seven beads again in the same direction and through the first bead for a third time. Pull tight to form a circle, leaving a 20 cm (8 in) tail. You will need this in Step 6.

2 Thread 16 size 10 transparent blue seed beads onto the longer end of the monofilament. Thread around the outside of the end bead then back through the next bead towards the circle. This forms the tip of the petal.

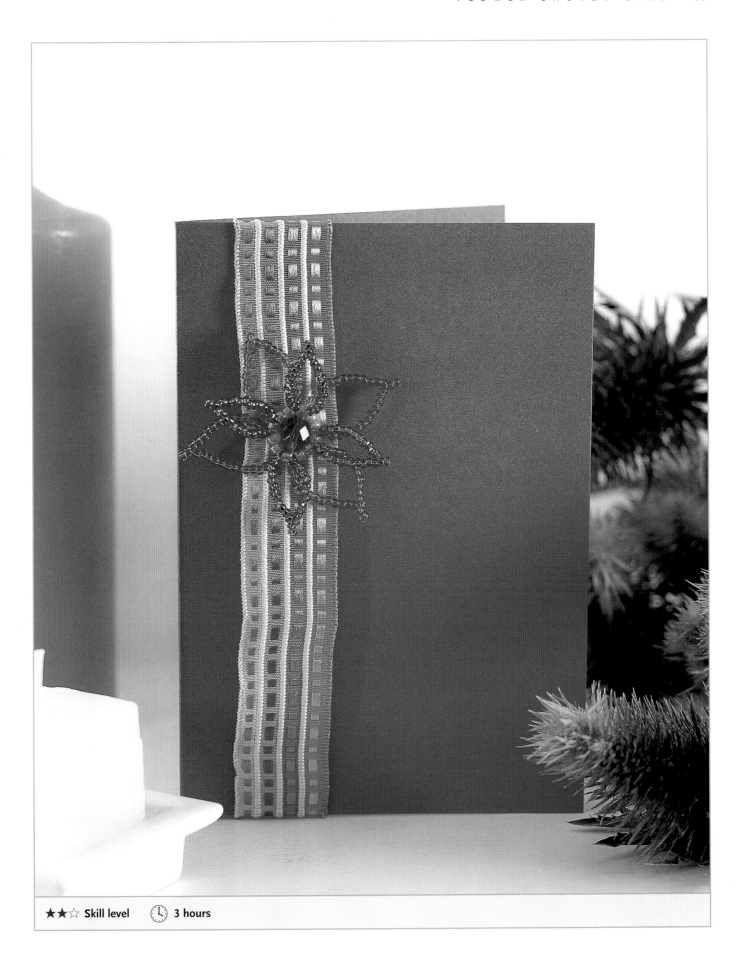

★★☆ **Skill level**   🕐 **3 hours**

3 Thread on 14 transparent blue seed beads. Starting two beads away from where the petal starts, thread back through (against the direction of the thread) five beads of the circle. Pull tight. This is the first petal.

4 Thread on 16 transparent blue seed beads. Take the thread around the end bead and then thread it back through the next bead. Add 14 more seed beads, and, starting at the size 7 bead two beads back from where the petal started, thread back through the last five beads. Repeat the steps until four petals have been made.

5 To make the inner petals, thread through the next size 7 bead in the circle. Thread on 14 size 10 silver-lined blue seed beads, take the thread around the end bead and then thread it back through the next one. Add 12 seed beads then thread back through the last size 7 bead. Thread through the next three seed beads in the circle.

6 Repeat Step 5 until four inner petals have been made. To add the centre of the flower, thread on an 8 mm faceted blue bead, then thread through the size 7 bead on the opposite side of the circle. Pass the thread back through the size 7 beads of the circle until it is next to the tail thread. Tie the two threads together using a reef knot. The flower is now complete.

Helpful hint
This project needs to be made with monofilament because it adds shape to the petals while going through the beads several times.

7 Neatly trim one end of a 50 cm (20 in) length of ribbon and dip it in glue to prevent fraying. Leave to dry. Measure the ribbon to the exact length for a choker, approximately 35 cm (14 in); however this does vary from person to person – if possible, do check in advance. Leave an extra 5 cm (2 in) then cut and treat the end with glue. Cut 4 cm (1½ in) of iron-on Velcro and, following the manufacturer's instructions, iron one side of the Velcro onto each end of the ribbon. Sew the flower onto the centre of the ribbon.

8 Wrap the ribbon round the card, using the Velcro to fasten on the inside of the card, to tuck it out of the way. The wire in the ribbon should hold it in place. If not, a strip of double-sided tape will secure it.

Helpful hint
If you struggle to get hold of monofilament, it is available at any fishing tackle shop.

Spiral rope bracelet

JEMA HEWITT

Spiral rope is one of the easiest but most rewarding bead weaving stitches, and as an added bonus it grows really quickly. This three-strand bracelet uses exquisite Japanese bugle beads to create a helter skelter type design. You could also use contrasting colours or different-sized seed beads instead of bugles for an alternative look.

"This project would be equally effective as a choker, so why not make a matching set? Do use Japanese bugles however, as Czech ones have sharp edges that will tear through the thread very quickly."

You will need

Materials

- 3 m (10 ft) turquoise Nymo D or Silamide thread
- 10 g size 9 seed beads
- 6 sterling-silver necklace ends
- 15 g Japanese bugle beads
- 4 x 3-hole spacer bars
- Sterling-silver three-strand clasp

Tools

- Scissors
- Size 10 beading needle
- Flat-nose pliers

1 Cut 50 cm (20 in) of Nymo D or Silamide thread and, using a beading needle, thread on one seed bead. Go through the bead again and tie a reef knot to secure it. Thread on a necklace end, positioned so the seed bead will be contained in it when shut. Thread on four seed beads and a bugle bead. Pass the needle up through the necklace end, through the seed bead, then back down through the necklace end and four seed beads.

Helpful hint
If you need to undo some work, unthread the needle and pull the thread through from the bead end. Don't try to pass the needle back up through the work.

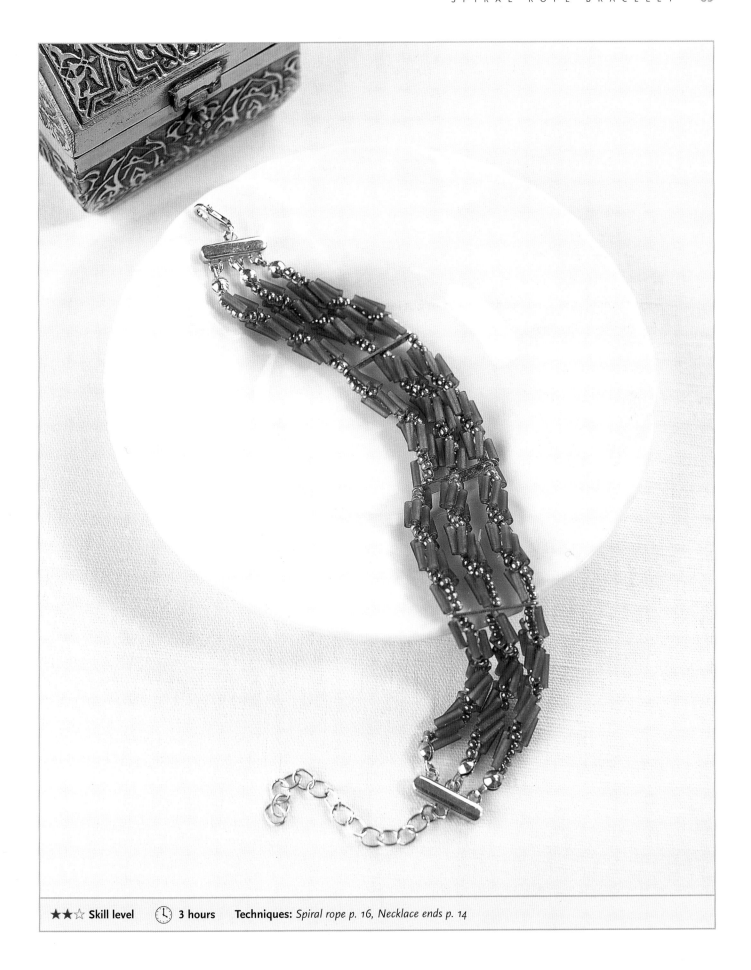

★★☆ **Skill level**   🕐 **3 hours**   **Techniques:** *Spiral rope p. 16, Necklace ends p. 14*

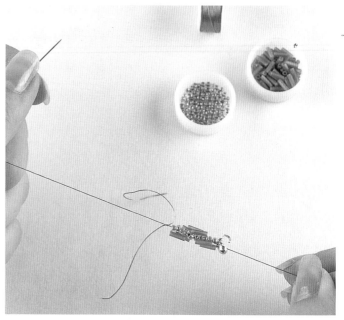

2 To start the spiral, add one seed bead and one bugle bead. Push them down to the others. Pass the needle up through the top four seed beads, leaving out the bottom seed (the one next to the necklace end). Arrange the second bugle so it lies to the right of the first bugle. You will see the beads begin to step up.

3 Continue adding a seed and bugle and passing the needle through the previous four seeds. Make sure each new bugle lies to the right of the one before or it won't spiral properly. If you need to add thread, leave a long end and tie a reef knot. Weave the two ends into the spiral very securely.

4 Repeat until you have added 18 bugles. Now thread on a spacer bar, four seeds and a bugle. Pass the needle back down through the spacer bar, through the last bugle and last four seeds, then back up through the spacer bar and top four seeds. Add a seed and a bugle and continue making the spiral as before. Repeat for another 18 bugles and add a spacer bar in the same way until you have three space bars and four sets of spirals.

Finish with 18 more bugles then thread on a necklace end followed by a seed bead. Loop back through the seed bead, down through the necklace end, through the top four seeds, up through the bugle and the necklace end and through the seed bead. Repeat this sequence a few times until it's secure.

Create two more strands in the same way. Pass the second strand through the centre holes of the spacer bar and the final strand through the bottom holes. Close the necklace ends very gently over the seed bead. Finally attach the necklace ends to the clasp with flat-nose pliers.

Variation

Other ideas

This choker is made from three rows of spiral rope with two lengths of beads in between. A single strand made from two sizes of seed bead makes a simple accessory.

Knotted pearl necklace

ROBIN BELLINGHAM

This three-strand knotted pearl necklace is a timeless classic. It has a simple elegance and doesn't necessarily need an occasion to be worn. Pearls have always been spaced with knots to prevent them chipping when knocked together while being worn. Another reason for knotting was so that you didn't lose very many if the necklace broke.

"Gimp or French wire is a finely spun coil of wire, which is used on the exposed thread at the clasp. Its primary purpose is to protect the thread from wear and tear so that the necklace lasts longer."

You will need

Materials
- 76 x 4 mm pearls (pre-strung)
- 68 x 5 mm pearls (pre-strung)
- 60 x 6 mm pearls (pre-strung)
- Headpin or stiff beading needle
- Gimp (French wire)
- Multi-strand or 3-strand clasp
- Glue

Tools
- Flexible beading needle
- Scissors

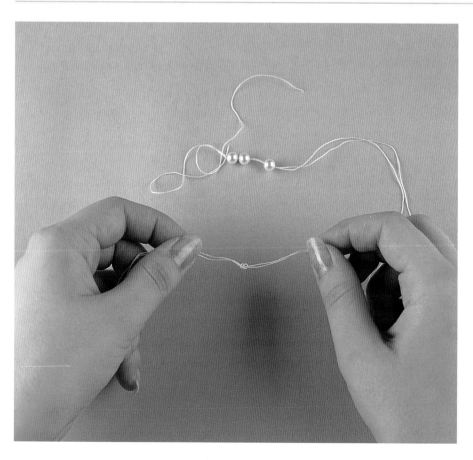

1 The three strands use three different sizes of pearl. Always tackle the smallest pearl strand first, this will set the length of the multi-strand necklace. The other two strands should hang lower each time in order to give the required effect. Pre-strung pearls are the most handy beads to use for this project. Tie a knot at each end of the strand. Separate the first three pearls from the majority and push to the end – you will need these at the end of the project when you come to attach the clasp. Leave a 30 cm (12 in) gap and then tie another knot

Helpful hint
For a quicker project make a single-stranded pearl necklace.

★★★ Skill level ⏱ 7 hours

2 Move one pearl from the majority up against the first knot you have tied. Now hold one hand flat and drape the pearls over your hand so that the three separated pearls are in front of your fingers and the majority of the pearls are hanging behind. The front pearls should hang below your hand. You should have a front thread and a back thread.

3 With your spare hand bring the front thread around behind the back thread and bring it up and over to the front of the second and third finger. Grip the thread with these two fingers.

4 Pull this thread so that your hand is pulling out of the loop you have just made. With a finger, pull this loose knot close to the pearl you are working with. Place a beading needle or headpin in the centre of the knot so that it doesn't tie itself together.

5 Use the needle to move the knot up against the pearl being held by the first knot. Once you have the knot as close to the pearl as possible, remove the needle and tighten the knot against the pearl.

6 Move another pearl from the majority up against the knot you have just tied and repeat from Step 3. Remember to regularly check the length of the strand you are knotting and that three pearls have to be left untied at each end to secure the clasp. Repeat this knotting procedure for the other two strands of pearls.

7 Cut six 1 cm (½ in) pieces of gimp wire.

8 Cut off the knot, holding the three loose pearls at one end of the strand. Push these three pearls against the rest of the knotted strand. Using a flexible beading needle, take the thread through one of the short lengths of gimp and then through one of the corresponding loops in a multi-strand clasp and finally through the first of the three pearls.

9 Pull the thread until the gimp is looped through the clasp loop and there is no gap in the thread between the gimp and pearl. Allow a very small gap between the three pearls for a knot.

10 Tie a knot by forming a loop around the necklace strand with the loose end and tucking it up inside this loop.

11 Pull tight and use your needle to thread through the next bead. Repeat again with tying a knot and thread through the third bead. This time you do not need to tie a knot but just cut the thread as close to the pearl as possible. Add a dab of glue to each of the two knots you have just tied.

12 Make the other two strands in the same way. Test the length by having the clasp closed together and holding the second strand's loose end through the corresponding clasp loop. If you need to add one or more beads then repeat Step 3–5 with the required number of beads. As long as you have one glued knot holding each end then that will suffice. Repeat Steps 8–11 until all three strands are complete.

Figure-of-eight earrings

ROBIN BELLINGHAM

This is the most challenging of my projects. I have made more earrings than I care to mention, using both machine-made and handmade components. I prefer to make earrings from handmade components, it creates totally unique earrings that can definitely be called "designer".

"It will take some practice, but I hope you'll agree the end result will justify the means."

You will need

Materials

- 2 x 15 cm (6 in) lengths of 0.8 mm (20 SWG) wire
- 2 x 20 cm (8 in) lengths of 0.4 mm (26 SWG) silver-plated wire
- 4 x 10 cm (4 in) lengths of 0.4 mm (26 SWG) wire
- 4 x 4 mm lapis lazuli semiprecious beads
- 2 sterling-silver fishhooks

Tools

- Pen
- Wire cutters
- Flat-nose pliers
- Round-nose pliers

1 Make two marks 1.5 cm (½ in) either side of the centre of one 15 cm (6 in) length of 0.8 mm (26 SWG) wire. Make a mark on the side of the pen and line it up with the one on the wire. Pinch together with thumb and forefinger, so that the marks are under the thumb. With your free hand, smooth the end of the wire nearest the mark you are using around the pen until the ends of the wire cross.

2 Repeat the same process to form the other loop in the opposite direction. When pinching the two marks together the first loop should point up. The ends of the wire that cross in the middle should be parallel to each other. Trim each end of the wire as close to the centre where it crosses as possible.

3 To make the centre, use one 20 cm (8 in) and one 10 cm (4 in) length of 0.4 mm (26 SWG) wire. Approximately one-third of the way down the longer piece, hold the shorter piece of wire against the longer one, leaving a 1.5 cm (½ in) tail on the shorter wire. Pull this tightly around the long wire three or four times to form a coil. Add a semiprecious bead to the longer wire and hold it next to the coil you have just made. Wrap the shorter wire once around the bead, then form a coil in the same fashion on the other side of the bead to secure it. Repeat this a second time to add another bead about one-third of the way from the opposite end of the same long piece of wire.

4 To attach the two pieces together, adjust the beads and coils to sit in the centre of each loop. Leave about 6 cm (2 in) at the bottom of the shorter piece of wire to wrap around the bottom loop. Wrap around the eight shape twice each side of the centre wire. Trim and tuck the end away with flat-nose pliers.

5 Secure the beaded wire to the centre of the figure-of-eight by wrapping it around three times. The first time you wrap it around the centre you will need to hold it in place. Once it's in place, you can wrap it around the second time and then the third time without holding it.

6 Wrap the wire over the top of the top loop, thread under and wrap twice more. To make a loop at the top for hanging, wrap the wire around one nose of a pair of round-nose pliers. Hold the pliers against the top of the figure-of-eight. Wrap once around the plier jaw and figure-of-eight and then twice more just around the figure-of-eight.

7 Trim and tuck the ends of each coil. Twist open the loop at the bottom of a fishhook and hang the figure-of-eight earring from the open loop. Close the loop with pliers. Repeat for the second earring.

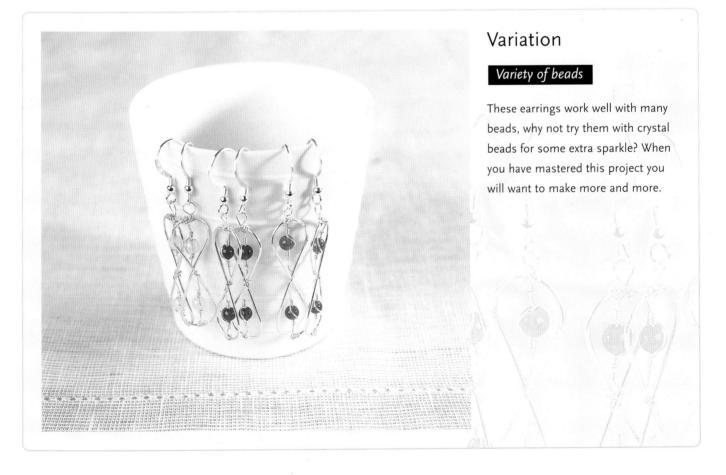

Variation

Variety of beads

These earrings work well with many beads, why not try them with crystal beads for some extra sparkle? When you have mastered this project you will want to make more and more.

Star choker necklace

HANA GLOVER

Stars and beads are two of my favourite things as anyone at our bead shop will tell you. This choker combines the two, and once you've made your first star it's surprisingly easy to do.

"Why not try other colours too, or make a matching belt with larger beads?"

You will need

Materials

- 1.5 m (5 ft) length of green Nymo D or Silamide thread
- Thread conditioner or beeswax
- Approximately 160 size 10/11 clear AB Delicas or seed beads
- Approximately 160 size 10/11 teal Delicas or seed beads
- Approximately 160 x 7 mm bugle beads
- Trigger clasp and tag

Tools

- Size 10 beading needle

1 Thread a beading needle with 1.5 m (5 ft) of Nymo D or Silamide thread. Press the thread against some thread conditioner and pull across to coat the whole length (this helps stop the thread knotting and fraying). Run the thread through your fingers to remove any excess.

2 Thread on two AB beads and one teal bead. Repeat until you have ten AB and five teal beads in a sequence. Push the beads to the end of the thread, leaving a 20 cm (8 in) tail. Thread through these 15 beads again to form a circle. Thread through the next two AB beads and one teal bead to secure.

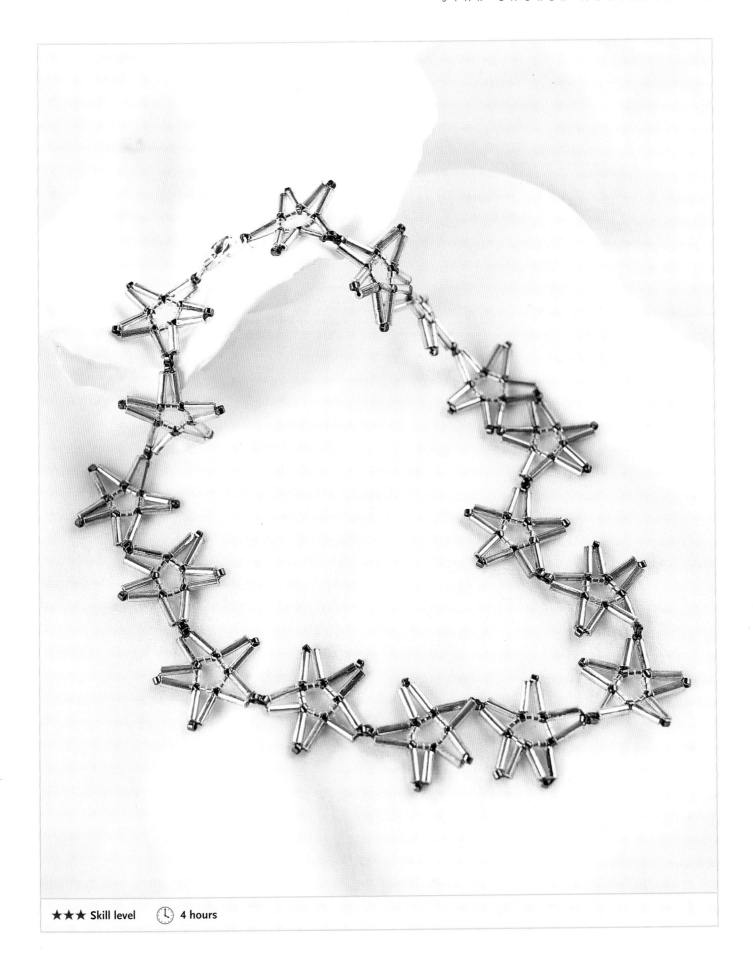

★★★ **Skill level**   🕐 **4 hours**

3 Add one bugle, one teal bead and one bugle. Thread through the next teal bead in the circle.

4 Add one bugle, one teal and one bugle. Thread through the next teal bead in the circle. Repeat the process until all five points are complete. Thread through the adjacent bugle bead towards the point of the star and through the teal bead on the point.

5 Add one teal and one bugle to form the point of the next star. Thread on one teal and two AB beads, repeating until there are 15 beads in the sequence. Form a circle by threading through 13 beads again, missing two AB beads.

6 Add one bugle then thread through the teal bead to form the first point. Thread down towards the circle through one bugle then the next teal bead. Continue adding points until the star is complete. Thread through the circle to the point where you wish to add the next star.

7 Continue adding stars until the necklace is the desired length. To add the trigger clasp, thread the needle through to the end of the point of the star where you want to attach the clasp. Thread on the clasp then back through the teal bead of the point to form a circle of thread. Repeat twice more to strengthen the join. Thread down the nearest bugle then knot around the thread. Thread through two AB beads then knot around the thread. Thread through the next teal bead then knot around the thread. Weave the thread through a few extra beads then cut.

8 Repeat the process at the other end of the necklace to attach the other side of the clasp.

Helpful hint

This necklace can also be made with all seed or Delica beads. The points are formed by missing the last bead and threading back through the next one.

Templates

↑ Embroidered bag (Full size) (pages 46–49)

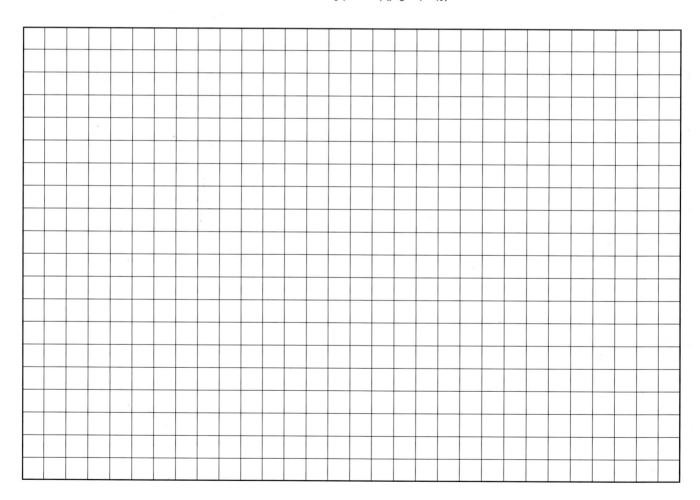

↑ A chart of blank squares for planning your own beadwork designs

Suppliers

UNITED KINGDOM

The materials and equipment used in this book can be found at your local bead shop. If you are unable to find what you need, please contact:

The Bead Shop
104–106 Upper Parliament Street
Nottingham NG1 6LF
Tel/fax: 0115 958 8899
Email: info@mailorder-beads.co.uk
www.mailorder-beads.co.uk

The following is a list of other useful suppliers:

The Bead Shop
21a Tower Street
London WC2H 9NS
Tel: 020 7240 0931
Mail order tel: 020 8553 3240
General bead supplies

Beads
259 Portobello Road
London W11 1LR
Tel: 020 7792 3436
General bead supplies

Constellation Beads
The Coach House
Barningham, Richmond
North Yorkshire DL11 7DW
Tel: 01833 621094
www.constellationbeads.co.uk
General bead supplies

Homecrafts Direct
PO Box 38
Leicestershire LE1 9BU
Tel: 0845 458 4531
www.homecrafts.co.uk
General wire supplies

H.S. Walsh & Sons Ltd
44 Hatton Garden
London EC1N 8ER
Tel: 020 7242 3711
Ring bending pliers, parallel pliers

Kernowcraft Rocks and Gems Ltd
Penwartha Road
Bolingey, Perranporth
Cornwall TR6 0DH
Tel: 01872 573888
Beads and hand tools

AUSTRALIA

The Bead World Warehouse
Bead World International
1/7 Villiers Drive
Currumbin
QLD 4223
Tel: 07 5534 1333
www.beadworld-international.com

Lincraft
Head Office
31–33 Alfred Street
Blackburn
VIC 3130
Tel: 03 9875 7575
General craft supplies, outlets nationwide

NEW ZEALAND

Bead Me Up
1184 Hinemoa St
Rotorua
Tel: 07 349 0844
Fax: 07 349 1082
Email: rozcraft@iconz.co.nz
www.craftwarehouse.co.nz

Beads & Pieces
297 Ponsonby Road
Ponsonby, Auckland
Tel: 09 376 1030
&
56 Broadway
Newmarket, Auckland
Tel: 09 529 5455
Beads and findings specialist

Bead Gallery
18 Parere Street
Nelson
Tel: 03 546 7807
www.beads.co.nz
Beads and findings specialist

SOUTH AFRICA

Bead Sales
223 Long Street
Cape Town
Tel: 021 423 4687
Mail order fax: 021 422 1773
General bead supplies

The Bead Shop
89 First Avenue
Melville, Johannesburg
Tel: 011 726 2911
Mail order service

FURTHER READING

Bead & Button magazine
www.beadandbutton.com

Beadwork magazine
www.interweave.com/bead

Index